BGT-101
Budgeting 101

A GUIDE TO BEING A MORE FINANCIALLY AWARE HBCU STUDENT

DeShawn A. Pennix

DISCLAIMER:

This distribution is planned to give accommodating and educational material. It is sold with the understanding that the creator and distributer are not occupied with rendering lawful, bookkeeping, restorative, or other expert administrations. The writer and distributer particularly disavow all duty regarding any obligation, misfortune, or hazard, individual, or something else, which is caused as a result, straightforwardly or by implication, from the utilization or use of any substance of this book. No move ought to be made exclusively on the substance of the book. All item names referenced inside this book are trademarks of their individual proprietors. None of these proprietors have supported, approved, embraced or affirmed this book. Continuously read all information given by the manufacturers' products or services label before utilizing them. The author and publisher are not responsible for claims made by the manufacturers.

© 2016 DeShawn A. Pennix. All rights reserved.

BGT-101

DEDICATION:

This book is dedicated to everyone who has supported me in my endeavors. I want to personally, thank you all for the love, it is greatly appreciated.

TABLE OF CONTENTS:

Introduction..................................v.

CHAPTER 1:
Friend to Friend.... Let's have a Real Talk..Pg. 8

CHAPTER 2:
The Company you keep... they ain't cheap..Pg.14

CHAPTER 3:
#Reallifegoals......................................Pg. 27

CHAPTER 4:
The infamous Budget........................Pg. 33

CHAPTER 5:
Saving to SAVE and Investing to INVEST... Pg. 45

INTRODUCTION

While attending Norfolk State University in 2010, I developed some negative financial habits that could have caused a whole lot of damage in my future if I had not changed my ways. Think about it...being at NSU was my first experience gaining independence. I had no one telling me when to clean up, go to class, or study. It was amazing! However, I was at every party, social event, shopping too much, and eating at every place the city had to offer, but at the Café' on campus that I was paying for. Those habits ended up leaving me with overdraft fees, arguments with my parents (because they wouldn't give me money when I asked for it), working long hours at my summer job, no savings, and a checking's account with minimal money in it. I later successfully scrambled for ways to make more money, but I still had nothing to show for it. It was not until I had an in-depth conversation with my family about the importance of financial management, and this consequently made me want to be more conscious about the decisions I make with my finances. I began reading a lot of books, articles, and picking the brains of my business professors and university administrators about money. That was when I learnt that making more money is helpful, but if you do not know how to effectively utilize and manage it, your finances will always suffer. Soon after, I learned to create a college friendly budget that was conducive to my goals of becoming a more financially responsible individual. I began to study my monthly finances and with time I started investing to make my money work for me. I've learned so much about living in college on a budget and thus, I've decided to share those lessons with you.

 I caringly named and wrote this book BGT101, for a couple of reasons:

BGT-101

1. While attending Norfolk State University (shout out to my Spartans), I had many friends including myself who picked up on the bad habits concerning finances.

2. Most of the beginners-level courses at Norfolk State University began in the number 100 or 101.

3. I want young black scholars to build effective financial management skills during and after college.

4. Also, to let you know that your financial decisions can help you or break you.

"Hope it awakens a more financially responsible you!"

CHAPTER 1
Friend to Friend....
Let's have a Real Talk

"Not keepin it real to a friend is being a disservice to a friend." - @shawnizm

So my friend, we are here because we have some things to discuss. And before anything, are you in the correct mindset to have this conversation with me? Because I am not happy with some of your financial decisions since we became homies. Now, as a disclaimer, I am not here to be your daddy or your momma. Parenting is a full-time job that I am not here to fulfill. I know you had discussions with yourself about how you are going be successful in life. However, I have not seen any action from a financial standpoint. Now I know we both had almost or the same number of birthdays, but I do know that being financially responsible is one of the things that we cannot play with as college students. I am your friend and I care about you dearly. This is a topic that we need to discuss now before life happens, because it will. I would be a disservice to you as a brother if I do not speak my mind about things that matter. Many people have so called friends around them but they are only there to steer you away from what you are destined to be. You already know being around me requires you to be great and I want to be that inspiration for you. I am not talking entrepreneurship, even though I do believe all my people should own something, but just being the boss of your financial life. Wouldn't it be dope to be financially literate while in college? I think so. So... let's get into some things that have probably occurred during the semester(s). You purchased this book because you have been spending in futility. Yes, you may be one of the 'flyest' people on campus but, being fly doesn't always help. I know you must look decent when you are going to class but who are you trying to impress? That outfit that you bought averaging over $200 dollars was not necessary. Your shoe game is poppin' but did you really have to spend $200 on a sneaker that will be re-released. Ever since I met you, I've never seen you miss a sneaker release date. You are always at the mall or online store spending a lot of money. Yet, you barely have money to buy your textbooks, you never have gas in your car, and you always want someone to spot you money for the club..... What's going on friend? Isn't it about time you started reevaluating yourself and your money? Huh, what do you think? I think it's time that you got it together and make a plan for yourself. Do you have any idea what you could have done profitably with the money spent monthly on frivolities? You could have started all types of businesses, you could have shopped more responsibly, or you could buy things you actually need for school. College goes by extremely fast and I think it's time you start thinking about your future. You never know, a rainy day may come, you may have some long-term goals such as purchasing a house, or you may have a short term goal such as treating yourself to something you really want. So with that being said, we are going to bond like friends have never bonded before. I am going to give you some suggestions that I learnt during my time as an undergraduate of the best historically black colleges. I understand attending an HBCU can be lit with the culture, parties, and people, but there should be some personal development. Below are guides that I believe will be the beginning of being a more financially responsible you

- Evaluating the friends, you keep around
- Setting your goals
- Create a realistic and accurate budget
- Prioritize Savings
- Invest your coins to make more
- Relationships & Money
- Affirmations & Tips to get you inspired

Now, know that this takes an open mind. If you not ready to have this conversation, then try again later. However, do not open this book until you are 100% ready. One of my biggest *pet peeve* is uncertainty. I know you may think I'm coming off a little strong, but let me reintroduce myself to you. I am blunt and straightforward and this is a characteristic most friends do not have. They will beat around the bush and not keep it funky with you. How many times has someone comfort you by feeding you some mess because they feared offending you or hurting your feelings? How many times have you been more hurt that a friend has lied to you rather than telling you the truth? Oh…ok! I am here to inspire and make you great! Grab a pen or pencil and get ready to write down some information that I think will be vital in the way of your financial management.

CHAPTER 2

The Company you keep... they ain't cheap!

"Ya Crew should be assets, not liabilities."

-@shawnizm

You thought this conversation about others was done? Think again, it's only the beginning. Have you ever heard that "You are the company you keep?" This statement is very much true, but do you want to know what else is true? The company you keep ain't cheap! In this chapter, we are going to discuss all types of company we sometimes keep that hurts us financially. That means you may lose a significant other, a buddy you been meaning to cut off, or you will finally stop hanging out with those associates you just made because they know you one of the cool ones on campus. Some people can be very toxic if you choose to associate yourself with them. Trust me, I've met people that I thought were my friends and came to find out that they were not. Get your revenge by being the best "financial you" you can be. People can say many things about you, but you might as well be financially knowledgeable living good in college right. Trust me… those likes you get on social media will not feel as good as somebody knowing that you are about your paper. Anyway, let's talk about the people you should watch out for and the people you should have in your circle.

Here are the people you need to get rid of:

    I.   The "What's the move" Friend

This is the friend that you only hear from when the Greeks or party promoters are having the *livest* party off campus. They only chop it up with you because you got some juice on campus. Usually they think hanging out with you is going to make their social life pop. Little do they know it won't! This is also the person who has no car and offers no gas money….ever. Then when you ask for gas their responses are, "I only got enough to get in the party… I got you next time." Next time comes and it's the same thing again. Yet, they buy drinks like it's going out of style and expect you to watch them when they get too lit. Next thing you know, your gas is on E and all the "What's the move" friends in your car ridin' around the city for free. Now you got to feel your gas tank up and you just asked your parents for money. Bank account looking at you crazy right? The week has not even started and you thinking about how long you can make your gas last. Those fools can be characters…… get rid of them suckers!

II.   "Yo… you hungry" Friend

This person is not exactly a bad friend, but you must be mindful of this friend and your money. You might have a couple of these friends in your group, which is a serious damage to your pockets. The "Yo… you hungry" friend hits you up during your school café hours or in the middle of the night because they are hungry. This friend may have a lot of disposable money because they work, parents support them, or they are on scholarship and receive a huge refund check from the university. This friend is always complaining about how disgusting the university food is, hence, this becomes the person you eat out with. You and your patna' are always at the poppin' restaurants and fast food spots. Then you realize you have spent hundreds of dollars in eating out over the months. Do yourself a favor, watch your expenses on food. I know you are on your school's meal plan! You need to implement a realistic food budget when in school (we will talk more about this later in the book).

    III.   The " Let's do something, but need to sit down somewhere" Friend

This friend needs some personal guidance as well…lol. Usually, this friend is always making plans for other people and not considering their lives and pockets! Anytime a break comes around from school, this is the one who wants to visit every city and state, but have no job. They live off their refund checks and does not utilize their full potentials to be great. Grades are always terrible, but never miss a campus event to save their soul. It's almost like they want to be seen by someone, or they are going to miss something happening in the world. You don't have to get rid of this friend, but be cautious and aware. Peer pressure is very real and you may sign up for trips, parties, or events that your pockets cannot afford this time around. Remember, watch the company you keep… they ain't cheap!

IV.   The "You should get it" Friend

Reading that subheading, you should already know what kind of friend this is. Have you ever shopped in a store for a specific item and after purchase and on way out of the store, you see something you want, but don't need. You look at the item and you are enticed to buy it. Then your friend that didn't buy anything says, "You should buy it!" They usually keep going with the words you wanna hear. They are in your ear telling you how cool you would be with that new phone or Jordan's. However, you know deep down you shouldn't buy it and that your remaining cash may be needed towards things you have to take care of. Like I said, peer pressure is so real… even when you are in college. Peer pressure so real, sometimes you don't even know you being peer pressured! Lol… be careful friend.

V. The "Bae...Boo...Sugar...Booger... Whatever you call them" Lover

Okay, so some of us have a better understanding when dealing with significant others. However, that's not the case for everyone. This lover is the one who never has anything to offer in the relationship. Your lover is always broke...no car or anything else. The bill of food is always paid by you and they are always mooching of someone. When your fridge is stocked with snacks they come to your dorm all the time! This is the lover who you always buy gifts for (good ones too) and when you think it's time for them to reciprocate the love, you don't get much or nothing at all.

Please do not get this person confused with someone who is grindin' day in and out to be someone great. The difference between the two is "initiative". If your significant other is not taking the initiative to do the needful. You may need to talk to your significant other and figure out a new plan. If they are not down for the cause, or can support you on your journey to being a financially responsible college student. You might need to tell them to bounce! Please don't get scared, if you want to be a great lover, they have to be one too. People break up all the time because of money. Again, mooching and being a broke lover can cause hindrance in your journey. If you are truly tired of seeing an open fist like the Gross Sisters on Proud Family.... get rid of bae!

Okay, I think I covered all the friends you should watch out for when you are in college. But I have some good friends to share with you that are excellent to keep in your circle. When I was obtaining my undergrad in business, I was able to meet some people who were great influences on me. Prior to attending college, the way media and sometimes our own advertised our people. I did not think it was possible to meet people who look like me and have unbelievable qualities that I want in myself.

These are the people you should keep in your corner when in your quest to being a financially responsible college student:

I. The "Business Minded" Friend

This is the best friend you can have in my opinion while attending an HBCU. This is the friend whose creativity is 'crazy'. Usually this person will always encourage their friends to become entrepreneurs themselves. This is the friend who supports you always at your engagements and graduations. These friends have the most mind blowing advice when it comes to finances and business. I'm talking about the "movers and the shakers" on campus. This is the person who pushing hundreds of dollars out of a small dorm room...lol. Seriously, I know a guy who was the number one campus barber on campus. I mean he had his clients sneaking in dorms just to get cut by him. I also have a good friend who started her own business out of her room at home. She created a Fraternity/Sorority apparel line that made her thousands of dollars a year. She is the real definition of a boss. I've gotten so much knowledge from her since meeting her in our business statistics class. If you do not have this type of friend, go to the business or fine arts halls of your college campus, which is usually where they hang out at. Pick their brain and get some information from them.

II. The " Never Jobless" Friend

Keep this friend around and close! This person always has some sort of job during the year and an internship during the summer. The "Never Jobless" friend can sell themselves to anyone. This person can give you interview pointers when it's time to find a job to stack your cash up. This person is always getting hired when it's time to graduate. RA's, Greeks, and Campus Leaders are the type of people who usually fits this description. So, now you know who to link up with in terms of employment. Pick their brain...its free information

    III.   The " Can I keep it 100" Friend

This is the friend who has probably seen a lot in life. The "Can I Keep it 100" friend probably does a lot of community work. You know... the pro-black kind of person. This individual has a lot of knowledge about how things work and an interesting perspective on the black experience. This person will have a lot of suggestions concerning the unconscious financial decisions African-Americans make. Therefore, you should utilize this person to help you with your decision making process when buying things you don't need. This friend will definitely let you know what you need and make sure you only have what you need! I met a couple of individuals who fits the description, if I did not meet those people. I may not be in tune with the social issues surrounding our community. But, keep this person around, they will serve as your Master splinter or something like that.

IV. The "Always there" Friend

This is a friend that you must never let go! Have you ever met someone who does not miss no one's graduation? Have you ever met someone who is always throwing a surprise party or baking someone cupcakes for their birthday? This is definitely that friend. This person is always there and ready for whatever. You should keep this person around because they will be of assistance emotionally and financially when necessary. The "Always there" friends usually are naturally giving people. Do not be afraid to ask for help when you need it! But, do not take advantage of them.

V. The "Hard to believe lover"

Okay, I'm back at it again with the love stuff. I briefly talked about this person in the book before. You know the person who may not have it all, but they are trying to succeed. Yea, that person. Well, I'm going to elaborate more on this person. This lover also is supportive and takes on some of the roles of all the friends I've already discussed. If this person is very supportive on your new journey of being a financially responsible person, they will learn new habits along with you as a way to support you. However, it will help you two together because hopefully your relationship goal is to become one. With all the bad influence we have with society concerning relationships it can sometimes be "Hard to believe" that you have someone who is truly supportive of you. Keep that person around!

Now that you have all the information concerning the people you should keep around or re-evaluate. Please be mindful of the people that are in your space. You may not actually think they hurt your pocket, but in the real sense of it, they actually do.

CHAPTER 3

#Reallifegoals

"Nothing more real than having some goals...get you some!"

-@shawnizm

In this chapter, we are going to discuss real-life goals and how it relates to being a financially responsible college student. In this chapter, you will see an example of a budget and the transactions that we placed within the budget. Once this chapter concludes, you should be able to learn how to budget at a beginner's level.

Now, what I mean by real life goals are realistic things in life that you want to achieve on your journey to becoming financially responsible. If you can see yourself doing it, it is very real and you need to write it down, record it, or whatever. Writing down your real-life goals will give you that *kick* you need to excel financially. Writing down your real-life goals will also encourage you and hold you accountable if you do not meet your goals. Be cool, do not get discouraged if you do not meet your goals. Just change the plan, but never the goal!

I challenge you to create a vision board and place all of your financial goals that you want to complete during college and even post-graduation. This board should reflect all your financial dreams and aspirations. If that means you want to buy a house for investment purposes. Draw or cut out a house and place it on the board. If you want to save 3,000 dollars in one year, draw 3,000 dollars on the board. Completing a vision board gives you a clear eye view on what it is you need to focus on and breathe life into your goals.

Here below is my financial vision board during my undergrad experience. It entails the things I wanted to accomplish during the duration of my undergrad career at an HBCU:

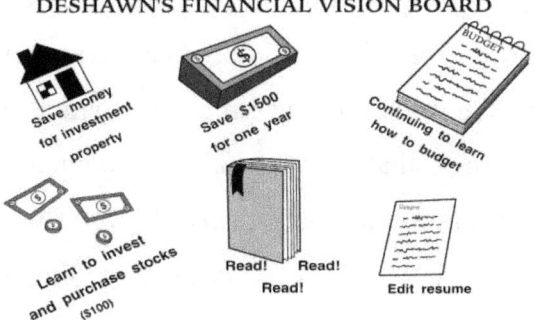

Everything within this illustration helped me financially of some sort. For example, the first thing I wanted to do was begin investing. After, receiving an investment account for Christmas and having conversations with my grandmother about the importance of doing meaningful things with my money. I learned that at my age and in college with no real responsibilities, it was time to start making my money work for me. I began researching what it meant to be an investor. I began investing with small amounts into companies that I was familiar with. The excitement I received seeing my money accumulate was amazing and even the fact that I owned pieces of major companies was almost like a dream come true. What you think about that? After one semester, I accumulated over a thousand dollars in investments. It took a lot of discipline and remembering my real-life goals. I knew that post-graduation I wanted something my future self could thank me for. Therefore, when you are thinking of your goals do things that you will be proud of in the future. This should be an easy task since you are getting education for the same reasons. So grab a pen and begin writing down some financial goals you want to accomplish. On the next page you will find a page to jot down your financial goals. If you want to take it a step further and create a financial vision board, make it look more official than mine so you can hang it in your dorm room. Give yourself realistic due dates to hold yourself accountable, do not get too upset if you do not make a goal. Remember, never change the goal, just the plan. I did not accomplish some of my initial goals, but I best believe my next plan helped me reach them. Your only competition is yourself.

Notes:

CHAPTER 4

The Infamous

Budget

"Learn to budget, or your accounts will never see any big figures"

-@shawnizm

Okay, here we are at the infamous budget chapter. Within this chapter I will give you basic information on how to create a budget for your money. I used this method during undergrad in order from draining my checking account. Keep in mind that this will require some discipline, patience, and understanding your spending habits when you begin tracking and making a month-to month budget. I am going to include a blank transactions and budget page for you to use for your personal budget. When you create your budget make sure you record every penny that comes out of your pockets. It's the only way to get an accurate snapshot of your finances.

First thing that needs to be done is looking at your finances. This means seeing what your actual monthly income is, seeing your transactions over the month, and what you would like to change. After this, record all of your expenses over the month. You probably will be shocked to see where your money goes to and how much money you have wasted.

Second, you need to create your budget and write the numerical figures from your transactions within the budget. This means that within your budget you will create categories that relates to you (food, transportation, gas, entertainment, etc.). Since we are in college, housing may not be something we include in our budget since some may live on-campus. Do not worry I will show you an example of a budget to give you a visual of what it should entail.

Third, you need to begin to live responsibly while in school. Again, it means not exceeding your budget categories. I know you still may want to party heavily and do what you want, but you must keep your eyes on the real-life goals you planned. You can still do whatever you want, but it must match your budget. When I was obtaining my undergraduate degree, my biggest issue was eating out. It broke my heart when I had to eat in the school cafeteria more frequently. However, my pockets got fatter.

Below is an example of a college student budget and transactions:

Monthly Transactions:	
Transfer to Savings Account	$80
Investment Transaction	$25
Club Getintoit'	$30
Gas Station	$15
Gas Station	$20
Wally World Groceries	$20
FootRoom	$125
Wally World Groceries	$40
BustYourSpeaker Subscription	$14.99
CutJive – Cash Purchase	$20
CutJive- Cash Purchase	$7
Jeanz And More	$65

So here is an example of transactions for this month. Those numerical figures will be examined to create a budget that matches your finances. Transactions are important because it tells you where your money goes and how you will construct your budget. Again, you will need to manually record every transaction for the month and place them within a budget. Please do no cheat yourself by not including any transactions. If you spent money using cash and not a debit card. Record it so your budget can be accurate as possible. When making a budget, use the 50/20/30 method when figuring out how much money use should spend per month on needs and wants. The 50/20/30 method basically means you should spend 50% of your income on things you must have every month. Those items include housing, transportation, groceries, and utilities. The 20% goes to savings and investing. This must happen every month no matter what. Matter of fact, when you get paid, this is the first payment you should make. The last 30% goes to entertainment purposes. This is the money you would use to have a night out in town. Those percentages are not set in stone, you can alter them to your liking if you are saving and or investing the minimum of 20% each month. I want to challenge you to make your savings/investing percentage higher in order to save more! Now let's get into the budget:

Monthly Income:			
	Expected	Actual	Difference
Income			
Clothing Store Job	$550	$575	+$25
Allowance	$75	$75	-$0
Total Income	$625	$650	+$25
Spending Budget:			
Savings/Investing			
Savings	$75	$80	+$5.00
Investments	$25	$25	-$0
Housing			
Utilities	$0	$0	-$0
Parking	$0	$0	-$0
Internet and/or Cable	$0	$0	-$0
Entertainment			
Movies	$10	$0	-$0
Music Subscritions	$15	$14.99	-$0.01

BGT-101

	Clubbing	$20	$30	+$5.00
	Concert			
	Transportation			
	Gas	$45	$35	-$10
	Food & Eating Out			
	Groceries	$50	$60	+$10
	Shopping			
	Clothing	$65	$65	-$0
	Sneakers	$100	$120	+$20
	Personal Care			
	Haircut	$20	$27	+$7.00
Total Spending Budget		$425	$456.99	+$31.99
Total Actual Income- Total Budget= Actual Ending Balance			$650-$456.99= $193.01	End of the month actual balance is $193.01

In the budget, you see that that this person did well for this month with effectively budgeting their money. In some of the categories he exceeded his max budget, but that is okay if you plan to continue mastering your budgeting craft. Some of the categories he/she did not max the budget to its full potential such as the savings category. However, this person managed to not spend $193.01 over the month. I hope this individual places the excess cash somewhere meaningful. Now remember that this is an example of a budget, meaning that these are not your numerical figures. Now that you understand how to budget your money properly take the time to review your transactions for last month and write down what you want to change about your spending. Also, think about your income and how you want to utilize the 50/20/30 method. Remember, the method percentages are not set in stone, change them to make your money work efficiently.

Notes:

Transactions for the month _____:	

BGT-101

Monthly Income:			
	Expected	Actual	Difference
Income			
Income Source #1_____			
Income Source #2_____			
Total Income			
Spending Budget:			
Savings/Investing			
Savings			
Investments			
Housing			
Utilities			
Parking			
Internet and/or Cable			
Entertainment			
Movies			
Music Subscriptions			
Clubbing			

Concerts			
Transportation			
Gas			
Car Note			
Car Insurance			
Food & Eating Out			
Groceries			
Shopping			
Clothing			
Sneakers			
Personal Care			
Haircut			
Uncategorized			
Organization Fees			
Total Spending Budget			
Total Actual Income- Total Budget= Actual Ending Balance			End of the month actual balance is

CHAPTER 5
Saving to SAVE and Investing to INVEST

"Savings is the stash... investments make the money bags."

-@shawnizm

I know I briefly discussed saving a tad bit, but I wanted to expand on it some more and give you some tips. A lot of college students do not save their money when being in college. I know before I became financially aware of my situation. Every time I had money in my pocket I felt the urge to spend it, which eventually led me to calling my folks every minute about money and having to work twice as hard during the summer to make up for the financial mistakes I made during the academic year. Being in college is the perfect time for you to save your money. You do not have a lot of financial responsibilities and if you do, it's not much compared to older adults who are stacked with many responsibilities. Also, you are young! If you start saving and investing your money now on a constant basis, do you know how much you can accumulate? Thousands...and thousands of dollars! Please do not be one of those students who feel that they do not need to save until they get their first salary job. So, throw that ideology out of the window and save now.

Why not stack as much money up during your college career? I promise if you begin saving your money now your future self will be proud of you. Oh, and don't touch your savings unless it is an emergency. Your investments... don't touch those until opportunity is no longer there. After that, invest in other opportunities.

Here are some tips to utilize when you are saving in college:

1. Utilize your meal plan included in your tuition, it will prevent you from eating off campus.

2. If your meal plan comes with money you can spend on campus, use that to purchase groceries and/or campus restaurants.

3. Save 20% of whatever money comes your way.

4. Shop where students can get discounts.

5. Attend campus wide events, its free knowledge and free food

6. Become a Resident Assistant, your housing and meal plan are usually free. It may come with a stipend or paycheck.

7. Sign up for a university sponsored trip, universities sometimes will give their students per diem when traveling. It's better to spend that money, right?

8. Share textbooks with friends. I know in college many professors did not use text books frequently. Just use your friends as needed… and share yours too!

9. Ask your self do you really need it? Whenever you see something that you want while shopping, just ask yourself the question.

10. Get to the club before 11, when it's free…lol. If the party is giving you an opportunity to get to the party for free. Get there on time please. Time is money. Your money!

In terms of investing, it can be intricate and easy at the same time. Investing is when you take your money and take a risk by investing it into companies and/or real estate in hope of profits. People invest their money because it works around the clock for them by appreciating and making more money. This method is mostly used for long term goals, but can be used for short term goals as well. Now, how can you invest in college? There are many financial institutions that allows you to open investment accounts with low to no minimums. Also, there are apps that now allow you to invest with spare change or little amounts like $5. I personally use an app called **Acorns.** The app allows you to round up your spare change and move it over into the stock market. You will then become a partial owner of your favorite companies. **Loyal3** is also another app that is college friendly when investing into the stock market. Both apps are easy to understand and set up and takes little knowledge on the topic at hand. Now, as mentioned before, investing can be complicated. However, if you are ready to invest while you're in college, which I recommend. Here are some tips you can use while investing as a college student:

1. Utilize the campus library and public library to learn about investing.

2. Research different financial institutions first before opening an account with anyone. See what everyone can offer you as an investor.

3. Diversify your portfolio. This means invest in different sectors of the market. Do no invest in the same type of thing over and over. Find different types of stocks to add to your portfolio.

4. Invest right about... now! Please do not wait to begin investing. Waiting will make you lose out on investing opportunities and thousands of dollars. You don't want that now, do you?

5. Pick the brains of your business professors. I guarantee one of the professors has some advice you can't turn down.

6. Take an investment course as an elective at your university.

I sincerely hope you will be able to break your financial yoke with all these tips.

And also, do not forget that Financial Management is the key to Life!

Acknowledgement

Mommy- Believe it or not, I have learned so much from you it's scary.

You may not believe me, but I am your twin...lol. Thank you for everything!

Grandma- You have given me so much information concerning investing and understanding money. Without your teaching this book wouldn't exist. Thank you for everything!

Dad- Good looks for always lookin' out.

You have provided me knowledge that only a wise man could give me. The best gifts you have ever given me.

My Friends and Supporters- You guys have been on this journey with me creating this book.

This book would not be here if it was not for you all giving me the encouragement to write it. Thank you all!

Find DeShawn Pennix

Instagram-

@shawnizm

Clothing Brand:

www.loyalkingdom.bigcartel.com

www.ingramcontent.com/pod-product-compliance
Lightning Source LLC
Chambersburg PA
CBHW061222180526
45170CB00003B/1115